VOTE
VOTE
VOTE

THE AUSTRALIAN GOVERNMENT
John Lesley
GOVERNMENT IN AUSTRALIA
REDBACK publishing

First Published 2025 by
Redback Publishing
Suite 6, 13a Narabang Way,
Belrose NSW 2085
Australia

www.redbackpublishing.com
orders@redbackpublishing.com

ISBN 978-1-761401-11-4

Author: John Lesley
Editor: Caroline Thomas
Designer: Redback Publishing

Original illustrations © Redback Publishing 2025
Originated by Redback Publishing

NATIONAL LIBRARY OF AUSTRALIA
A catalogue record for this book is available from the National Library of Australia

CONTENTS

What is a Government? 4
Democracy 6
The Westminster System 8
Separation of Powers 10
Political Parties 12
Public Servants 14
Capital Cities 16
Levels of Government 18
Why Does Australia Have a King? 26
Republic or Monarchy? 28
What Name is Correct? 30
Glossary 31
Index 32

WHAT IS A GOVERNMENT?

A government is an organisation that is responsible for governing a group of people who are in a defined area.

The Australian Parliament governs the whole of Australia, each State Parliament governs its own State, and each Territory Parliament governs its own Territory. Local councils govern their own local government area.

Government and Opposition

When people are elected to the Australian Parliament, the group of them with the highest number in Parliament becomes the Government. They are responsible for making and changing laws for all Australians. The group with the next highest number of members becomes the Opposition. The role of the Opposition is to oppose the Government. The Opposition represents a large number of voters who did not vote for the Government.

This system ensures that even those who may not approve of the policies of the Government, still get to have a say in Parliament as long as their representatives have gained enough votes to be elected to represent their electorate.

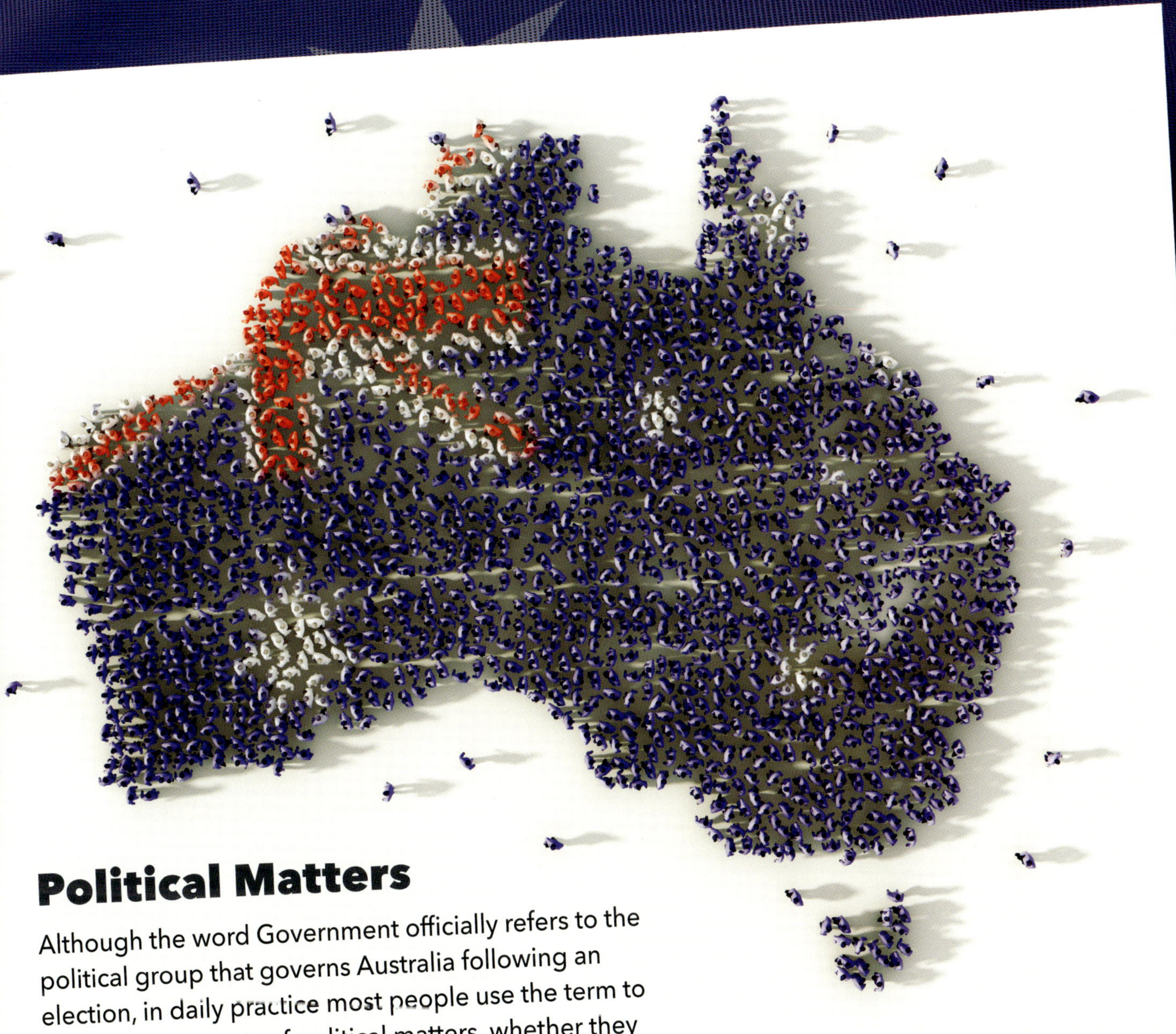

Political Matters

Although the word Government officially refers to the political group that governs Australia following an election, in daily practice most people use the term to refer to any aspects of political matters, whether they involve party politics or not.

Parliament House, Canberra

Question:

Are a government and a parliament the same thing?

Answer:

No. In Australia, the word Parliament refers to all the elected people in the Senate and the House of Representatives, from all parties, as well as the Monarch (represented in Australia by the Governor-General). The word Government refers only to the elected representatives who won the last election, and who work through government departments to put the policies of their Government into action.

DEMOCRACY

Representational Democracy

Not all democracies around the world operate in exactly the same way. In Australia, the form of government is called a representational democracy. This means that the people themselves do not all have an individual say in Parliament. Instead, citizens vote for the people who represent them in Parliament.

King Charles III and Queen Camilla

Monarchy

As well as being a representative democracy, Australia is also a constitutional monarchy, since the King or Queen of the United Kingdom (UK) is also the Head of State of Australia.

POLITICAL RIGHTS

Australians are proud to live in a country where citizens have the right to vote in free and secret elections for the people they want to act on their behalf in Parliament.

Political rights in Australia include:

Vote

The right to cast a secret vote in free elections

Voice

The right to voice a political opinion

Public

The right to take part in public meetings

India is the world's largest democracy

Direct Democracy

A direct democracy occurs when every person has a say on everything. This is the sort of voting you might do if you are deciding which movie to go and see with your friends. The choice with the most votes wins. Direct democracy does not work well when there are millions of people voting, and the government is large and complex.

World's Largest Democracies

The countries with the three largest democracies in the world are India, Indonesia and the USA.

Party
The right to join a political party

Religion
Freedom of religion

Press
Freedom of the press (media)

Union
The right to join a trade union

Speech
Freedom of speech

THE WESTMINSTER SYSTEM

Houses of Parliament, Westminster, England

Parliamentary Democracy

The Westminster System describes a parliamentary democracy that is based on the type of government that exists in Britain, Australia, New Zealand and Canada. The name comes from the area in London where the UK Parliament is located.

King Charles III

The USA and a number of other countries have forms of government that are derived from the Westminster System, but they have a president rather than the British Monarch as their Head of State.

Westminster System Guide in the NSW State Government

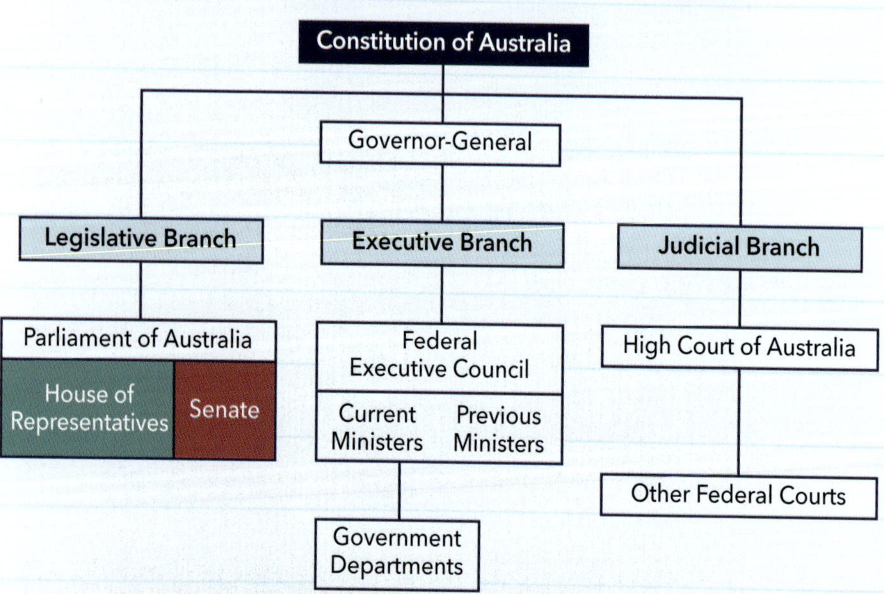

Commonwealth of Australia Constitution Act.

AN ACT

TO

Constitute the Commonwealth of Australia.

Cap. 12 [9th July 1900]

Features of the Westminster System in Australia

The Australian Parliament, as well as the State and Territory governments, operate in various ways that are all based on the Westminster System of government:

Head of the Government

The Monarch through their local representative, (in Australia the Governor-General), is advised by the head of the government.

Upper House

There is usually an upper house of parliament.

Lower House

There is an elected lower house of parliament.

Law Courts

The law courts are independent of the government.

Separation of Powers

There is a Separation of Powers to stop any one group from gaining absolute political power.

SEPARATION OF POWERS

The System

The Australian Government operates within a system called the Separation of Powers. In this system, the Parliament, the Executive and the Judicial system all have a separate role to play in the making and application of laws. This reduces the risk that any one group of people could hold too much power.

Political Influence?

In some nations, politicians seek to influence the way courts make decisions on whether a person has behaved illegally or not. In theory, this is not acceptable in Australia because of the importance placed on upholding the Separation of Powers.

Three Sections of Government

The three sections of the Australian Government provide a system that has developed with the aim of stopping either the Monarch or any one political party from gaining absolute power over the Nation. Each section is independent of the other and can make its own decisions on government matters for which it is responsible.

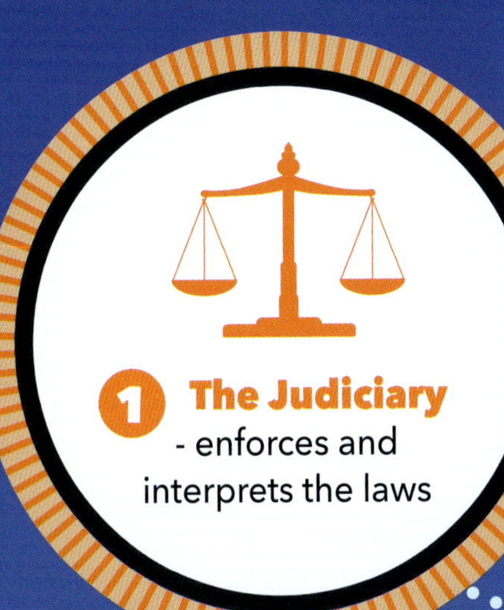

General Sam Mostyn, the 28th Governor-General of Australia

The Governor-General

Outside of these three levels of government in Australia is the Governor-General, who represents the Head of State, the British Monarch.

POLITICAL PARTIES

Similar Beliefs

Political parties are groups of people who have similar beliefs about how Australia should be governed. The grouping of elected representatives into parties is an important aspect of parliamentary government in Australia and of the Westminster System of government.

Members of political parties who are elected to either House of Parliament act together to have the views that they share made into laws.

Party Choice

People who are elected to the Australian Parliament can stand for election as independents, members of minor parties, or as members of one of the two main parties.

The two main parties in the Australian Parliament are:

- Australian Labor Party
- Liberal Party of Australia in coalition with The Nationals, often simply called The Coalition

They generally form either the Government or the Opposition in Parliament.

Minimum Membership

A political party can still exist even if none of its people are elected to any parliament. Once it does have elected members, it is called a parliamentary party. There must be at least 1,500 citizens who have joined the political party before it can be officially registered with the Australian Electoral Commission.

Branch Meetings

Political parties hold branch meetings in their communities. A member of the community can usually attend a branch meeting if they are interested in joining or finding out more about the party.

Independents

An independent Member of Parliament or Senator can never expect to become Prime Minister, since this role is reserved for the leader of the party which has the highest number of elected Members in the House of Representatives. Despite this, independents can sometimes hold a lot of power in Parliament. This is particularly the case when the Government is in power by a very small margin and therefore relies on the votes of independent Members to get new legislation passed into law.

PUBLIC SERVANTS

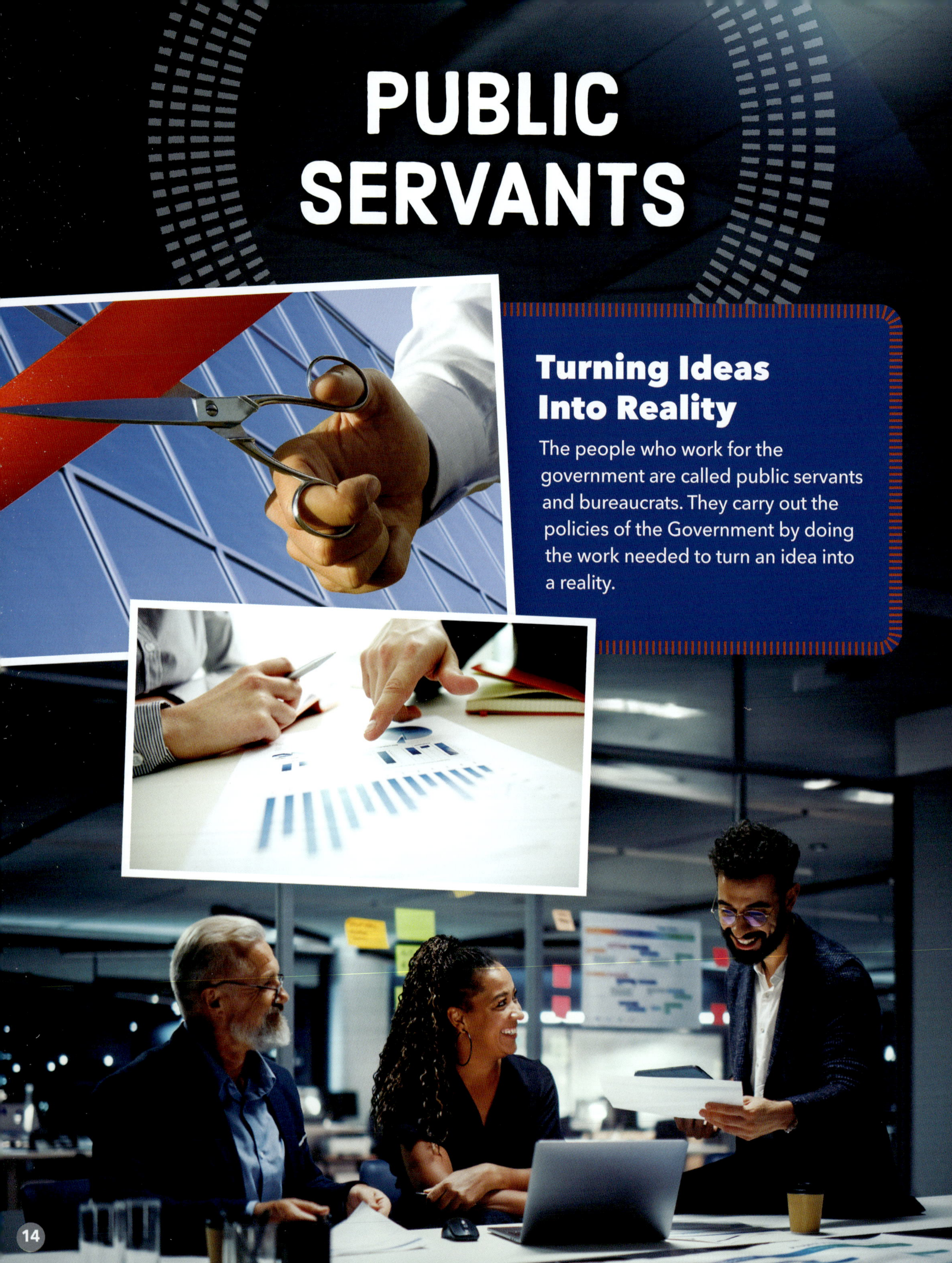

Turning Ideas Into Reality

The people who work for the government are called public servants and bureaucrats. They carry out the policies of the Government by doing the work needed to turn an idea into a reality.

The Australian Embassy in Washington DC, USA

VISAS

Global Work

The Australian Parliament is in Canberra, but Australian government offices and their staff work all around Australia, as well as in other countries where Australians need to have some official representation. Examples of the Australian Government at work overseas occur in embassies and trade offices all around the world.

Without Bias

Public servants are supposed to perform their duties without showing any bias that might come from whatever their own political ideas might be. Their role is to action the policies of the elected Government for which they work.

CAPITAL CITIES

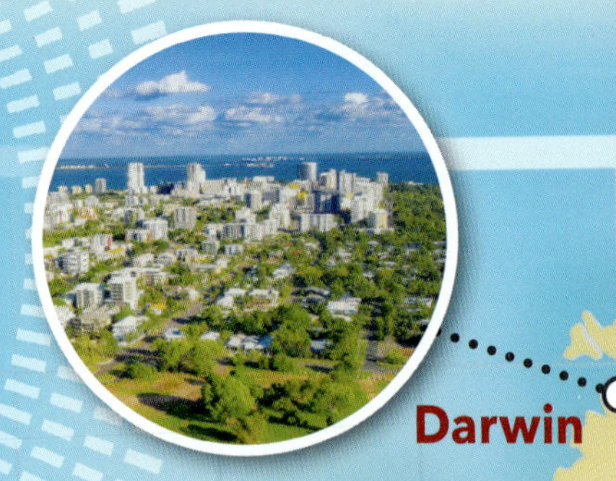

Darwin

Western Australia

Australia's Capital

Canberra is the capital city of Australia because it is the location of the Australian Parliament. A capital city is usually the location of the nation's government and main administration centres.

Perth

Parliaments in Foreign Exile

In countries where there is conflict about who will be in control of the government, a 'parliament in exile' may be set up in a city in another country, until the situation in the homeland changes and it is safe to return.

Capital Cities

The capital cities in each of Australia's States and Territories have their own parliaments and centres of government administration.

The official opening ceremony of Old Parliament House in 1927

The Youngest Capital City

The capital city is not always the largest or oldest city in a country. In Australia, all the State capital cities are older than Canberra, which only dates from 1913.

Northern Territory

Queensland

South Australia

Brisbane

New South Wales

Adelaide

CANBERRA

Sydney

Victoria

Melbourne

Australian Capital Territory

Tasmania

Hobart

LEVELS OF GOVERNMENT

There are three types or levels of government in Australia:

1 The Australian Parliament

2 Six State Parliaments and two Territory governing bodies (called Legislative Assemblies)

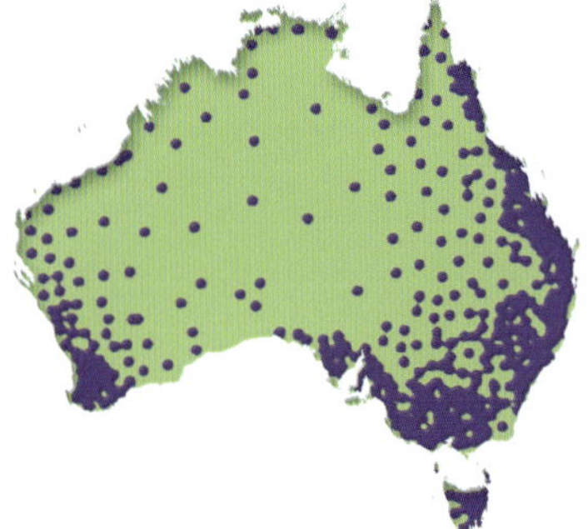

3 Over 530 local council governments

All three levels of government have elected representatives who make decisions, laws and rules for the people in their area.

The Australian Lower House

Unicameral and Bicameral

Having one house of parliament is called a unicameral system. Having two houses is called a bicameral system. The Australian Parliament has a bicameral system led by the Prime Minister.

The Australian Upper House

AUSTRALIAN PARLIAMENT

(based in Canberra, Australia's capital city)

Parliament's Responsibilities

The Australian Parliament is responsible for matters that involve Australia's relationship with other countries, or services that exist across Australia, such as postal services, income taxation, Federal social services, and Federal highways.

Laws made by the Australian Parliament can override laws or rules made by the other two levels of government in Australia.

STATE AND TERRITORY GOVERNMENTS

(based in the capital city of each State or Territory)

Second Level of Government

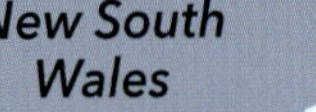

Local Transport

State and Territory Responsibilities

Hospitals, school education, police and local transport are the responsibility of State and Territory governments.

State Parliaments

Five of the State parliaments have two houses of parliament. Along with the two largest territories, Queensland has only one house, the Legislative Assembly.

AREA	TYPE	HEAD	HOUSES	GOVERNOR
Australian Capital Territory	Unicameral	Chief Minister	Legislative Assembly	No
New South Wales	Bicameral	Premier	Legislative Assembly Legislative Council	Yes
Northern Territory	Unicameral	Chief Minister	Legislative Assembly	Administrator
Queensland	Unicameral	Premier	Legislative Assembly	Yes
South Australia	Bicameral	Premier	House of Assembly Legislative Council	Yes
Tasmania	Bicameral	Premier	House of Assembly Legislative Council	Yes
Victoria	Bicameral	Premier	Legislative Assembly Legislative Council	Yes
Western Australia	Bicameral	Premier	Legislative Assembly Legislative Council	Yes

Leaders

The leader of a State government is called a Premier, and the leader of a Territory government is called a Chief Minister.

LOCAL GOVERNMENTS

(based in each main city of the local government area)

Third Level of Government

Local Government Responsibilities

Local governments are also called local councils, municipalities or shires. They are responsible for looking after local roads, libraries, garbage collection, parks and local halls. Many local councils also choose to make decisions on matters that are broader in scope.

Debating the Future of Local Councils

Local governments exist through State laws that explain how they are to be set up and how they may operate. They are not described in the Australian Constitution. From time to time, some people use this lack of constitutional recognition to suggest that local councils could be abolished and that their responsibilities could be transferred to State or Territory governments.

Greg Conkey, former Mayor of Wagga Wagga, New South Wales

Clover Moore, the longest serving Lord Mayor of Sydney

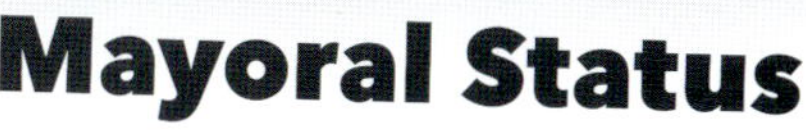

Mayoral Status

The leader of a local government body is called a Mayor, and the elected members are called Councillors. If the local government looks after a large or capital city, the leader might be a Lord Mayor. Having lord mayoral status is a privilege that is granted by the Monarch through the Governor-General, and only happens in very rare and special circumstances.

Council Numbers

There are more than **530** local council governments across Australia

SMALL TERRITORIES

Australia has eight other territories, some of which are unpopulated, or which have a limited level of local representation

Ashmore and Cartier Islands

Christmas Island

Coral Sea Islands

Heard Island and McDonald Islands

Norfolk Island

Norfolk Island, in the Pacific Ocean, is very remote and isolated from the mainland of Australia. In 2015, an Act of the Australian Parliament brought Norfolk Island under mainland responsibility and provided for the establishment of a Norfolk Island Regional Council to look after local services.

WHY DOES AUSTRALIA HAVE A KING?

Constitutional Monarchy

Since the Head of State in Australia is the British Monarch, currently King Charles III, the Australian Government is not only a representational democracy, but it is also described as being a constitutional monarchy. The Monarch cannot make decisions according to their own wishes and must follow the rules laid down in the Australian Constitution.

An Independent Nation

The nation of Australia was created on 1 January 1901, when the six separate British colonies joined together to form the Commonwealth of Australia.

The new country of Australia became an independent nation that remained part of the British Empire and had the British Monarch as its Head of State.

Well over a century later, there is no longer an Empire, but King Charles III, the British Monarch, is still the Head of State of Australia.

King Charles III

Royal Succession

King Charles III became the King of Australia on the death of his mother, Queen Elizabeth II, on 8 September 2022.

The British public pay their respects to the late Queen Elizabeth II

REPUBLIC OR MONARCHY?

Departmental Heads of the Australian Commonwealth Public Service, 1901

Ongoing Debate

Even before the Commonwealth of Australia came into being in 1901, there were discussions in the community about whether the new nation of Australia should remain a monarchy or become a republic, like the USA. These debates have continued until the present day.

The 1999 Referendum

The referendum of 1999 asked voters whether they wanted to make a change to the Australian Constitution to move from being a constitutional monarchy to a republic. The answer was no.

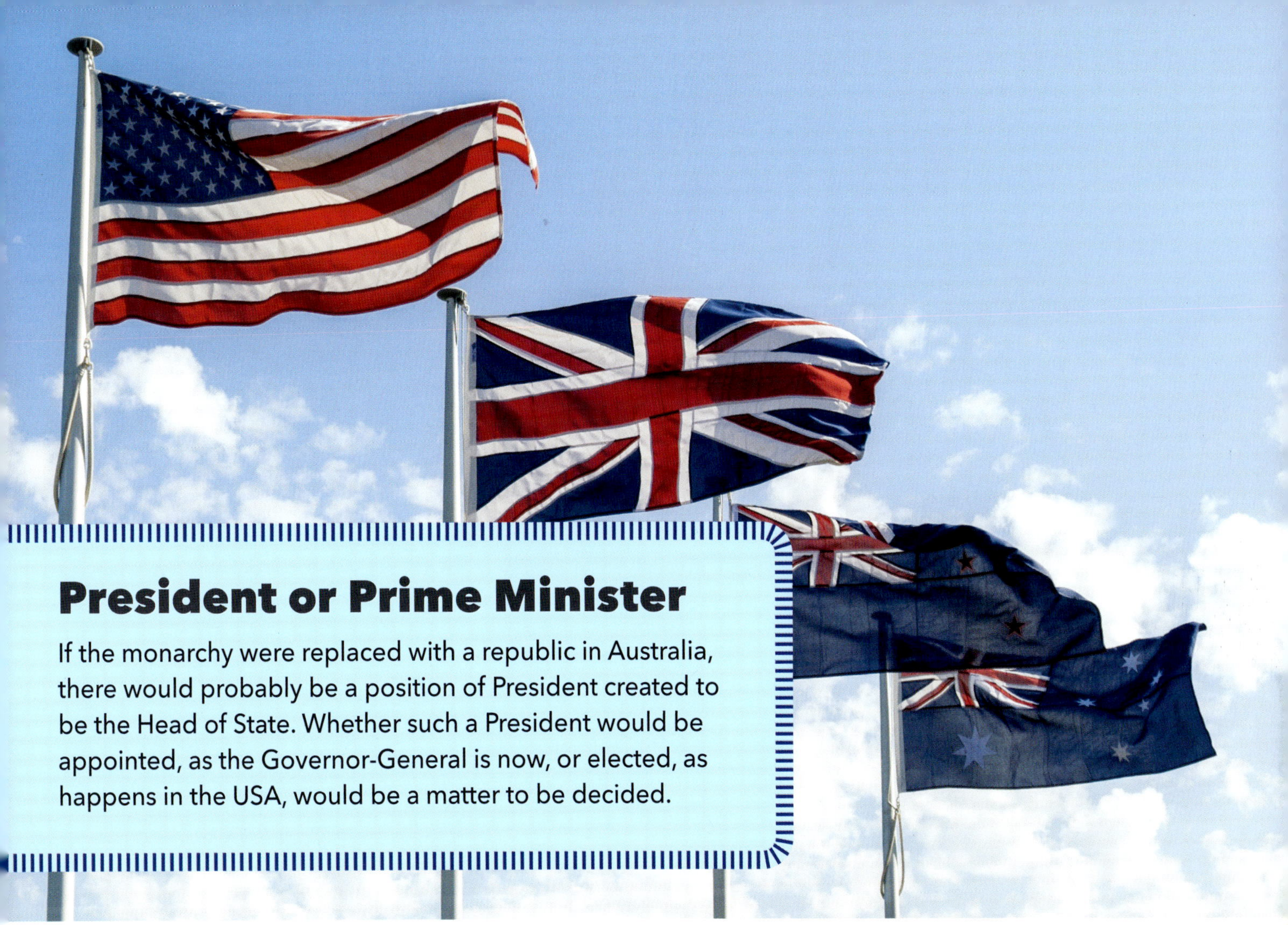

President or Prime Minister

If the monarchy were replaced with a republic in Australia, there would probably be a position of President created to be the Head of State. Whether such a President would be appointed, as the Governor-General is now, or elected, as happens in the USA, would be a matter to be decided.

New Logos

A new republic would require new logos throughout the country in thousands of locations. The term 'Royal' would no longer apply to defence forces such as the RAAF and RAN.

There are many arguments for and against changing Australia from a monarchy to a republic, and the debate about it still continues.

WHAT NAME IS CORRECT?

Australian people refer to their national government by a number of terms:

- **Australian Government**
- **Commonwealth Government**
- **Federal Government**

The Nation

At the founding of Australia, the official name given to the new nation in the Constitution was:

The Commonwealth of Australia

We now only use this formal term in official documents. Most of us just use Australia as the name of the country and the Nation.

Brisbane celebrates the foundation of the Australian Commonwealth in 1901

GLOSSARY

abolish .... get rid of

bias .... prejudice

bureaucrat .... public servant who does office work

citizens .... members of a country with rights to its benefits and with responsibilities to perform certain duties

constitutional .... referring to a constitution

interpret .... explain

judicial .... referring to a legal system

margin .... amount by which something is near its limit

Opposition .... party with the second largest number of elected representatives in parliament

override .... have the power to change

policies .... group of ideas to be put into action

politics .... system by which the wishes of different groups result in the activities of a government

privilege .... special rights not provided to everyone

registered .... officially listed

INDEX

Norfolk Island

Australian Electoral Commission 13

Constitution 6, 23, 26, 28, 31

Executive 10, 11

Governor-General 5, 8, 9, 11, 23, 29

Head of State 6, 8, 11, 26, 29

Houses of Parliament 5, 9, 12, 13, 18, 21

Judiciary 10, 11

Mayor 23

Monarchy 5, 6, 8, 9, 11, 23, 26-29

Opposition 4, 12, 31

States 4, 9, 16-18, 20, 21, 23

Territories 4, 9, 16, 17, 20, 21, 23-25

UK 6, 8

unicameral 18, 21

USA 7, 8, 15, 28, 29

Parliament House, Canberra

Acknowledgements

Abbreviations: l–left, r–right, b–bottom, t–top, c–centre, m–middle

We would like to thank the following for permission to reproduce photographs (images © Shutterstock unless otherwise stated): p2tl FiledIMAGE/Shutterstock.com, p3tl https://commons.wikimedia.org/wiki/File:Official_Programme_-_The_Commonwealth_of_Australia_Inaugural_Celebrations_at_Sydney,_Government_of_New_South_Wales,_1901.jpg, p3bl ChameleonsEye/Shutterstock.com, p6tr Michael Tubi/Shutterstock.com, p7tr cornfield/Shutterstock.com, p8br National Archives of Australia, Public domain, via Wikimedia Commons, p8tr Heide Pinkall/Shutterstock.com, p9mtr EQRoy/Shutterstock.com, p9ml FiledIMAGE/Shutterstock.com, p11br attribute gg.gov.au, p13ml GillianVann/Shutterstock.com, p13tr Sheila Fitzgerald/Shutterstock.com, p15tr https://commons.wikimedia.org/wiki/File:Australian_Embassy_at_night.jpg, p16tr https://mildenhall-origin.moadoph.gov.au/photo/943, Public domain, via Wikimedia Commons, p16bc Ikonya/Shutterstock.com, p18bl FiledIMAGE/Shutterstock.com, p19br FiledIMAGE/Shutterstock.com/Shutterstock.com, p19br FiledIMAGE/Shutterstock.com, p30tl FiledIMAGE/Shutterstock.com, p22br doublelee/Shutterstock.com, p23tr stock_photo_world/ Shutterstock.com, p23ml Bidgee, CC BY-SA 3.0 AU <https://creativecommons.org/licenses/by-sa/3.0/au/deed.en>, via Wikimedia Commons, p23mr Hpeterswald, CC BY-SA 4.0 <https://creativecommons.org/licenses/by-sa/4.0>, via Wikimedia Commons, p24tl Contains modified Copernicus Sentinel data 2021, Attribution, via Wikimedia Commons, p24bl Richard Ling, CC BY-SA 2.0 <https://creativecommons.org/licenses/by-sa/2.0>, via Wikimedia Commons, p24br Tristannew (original)Derivative: SHB2000 (cropped), CC BY-SA 4.0 <https://creativecommons.org/licenses/by-sa/4.0>, via Wikimedia Commons, p26br https://commons.wikimedia.org/wiki/File:Official_Programme_-_The_Commonwealth_of_Australia_Inaugural_Celebrations_at_Sydney,_Government_of_New_South_Wales,_1901.jpg, p27tr Lwsi CoxShutterstock.com, p27tl Howard Cheng/Shutterstock.com, p27bl V9 Media/Shutterstock.com, p27br Alexey Fedorenko/Shutterstock.com, p28tl See page for author, Public domain, via Wikimedia Commons, p29bl Adwo/Shutterstock.com, p30bl Tosca, Public domain, via Wikimedia Commons

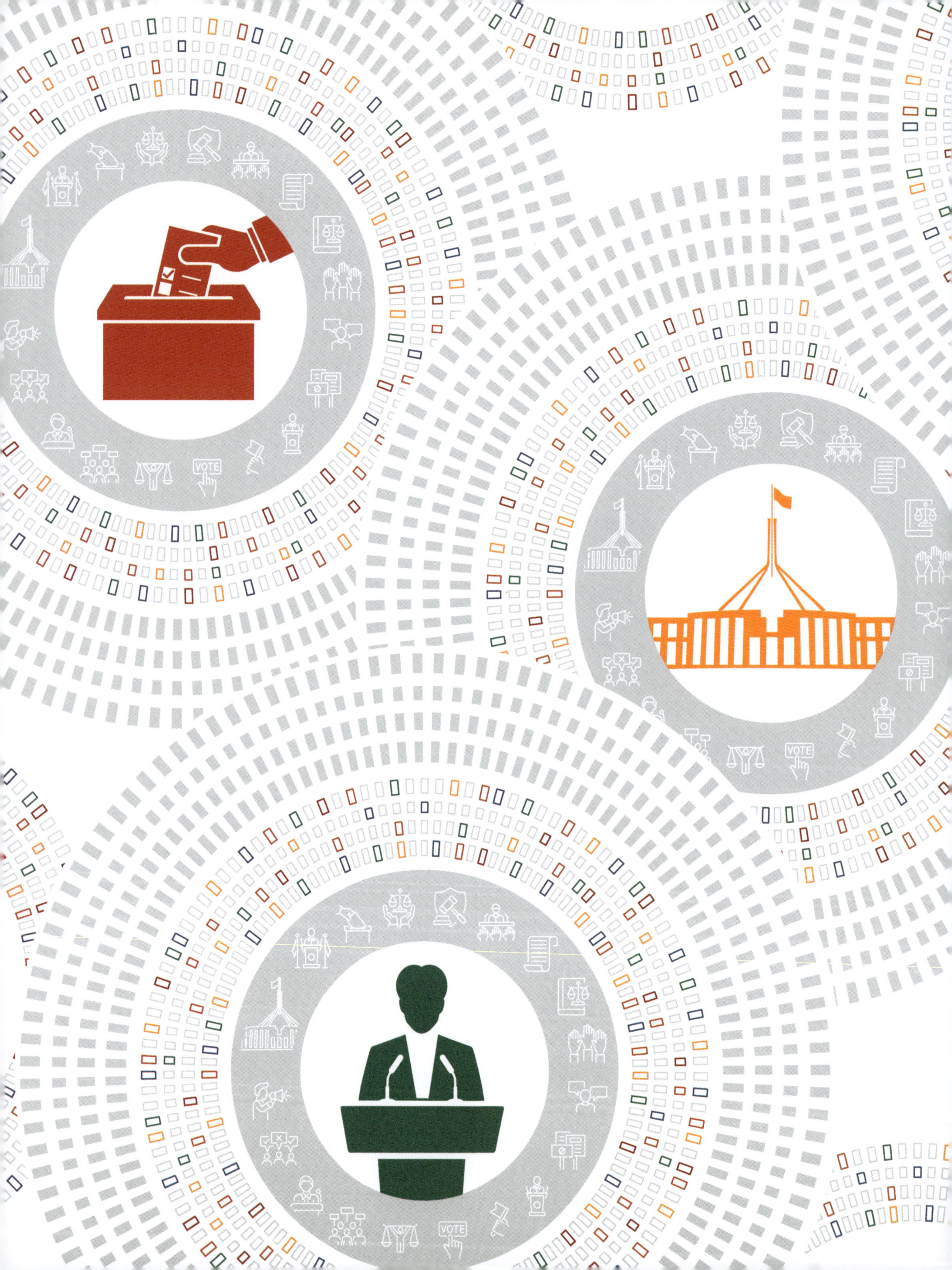
VOTE
VOTE
VOTE